Folksongs from India

selected and arranged by

PETER GRITTON

© 1993 by Faber Music Ltd
First published in 1993 by Faber Music Ltd
3 Queen Square London WC1N 3AU
Illustrations © 1993 by John Levers
Cover illustration by Angela Dundee
Music typeset by Silverfen
Printed in England
All rights reserved

ISBN 0 571 51372 7

Preface

In folksongs the earth sings; the mountains – they all sing; rivers, crops, festivals and processions, seasons and traditions – everything sings. (Mahatma Gandhi)

The wealth of musical material available for this collection is both huge and startlingly diverse. It has been impossible to represent all types of folksong, but it is hoped that the collection offers at least a glimpse of a musical culture far removed from our own in Europe and the West.

There has been civilisation in the subcontinent of India for at least 4,000 years. Since about 2,000 years ago Buddhism and Hinduism have been the predominant religions. An influx of Arabs, Turks and Afghans from the north and west about 900 years ago saw the introduction of Islam. Although worshippers of Islam (Muslims) were dominant in India 500 years ago, Hinduism and Buddhism thrived alongside. Today, we see a wonderfully rich and varied culture – music, drama, art, poetry and dance – drawn from all three ancient traditions.

In India, the music of the higher castes is known as 'classical' music, and has evolved through courtly life. The music of the lower castes is folksong – the music of the people – and has been passed down aurally through the generations. It is generally understood, however, that in India *all* culture brings people closer to God, and you will notice that many of the songs in this collection contain references to gods and goddesses. Although 'folk' and 'classical' styles are very different from each other, there are some fundamental musical characteristics common to both.

Performance

Wherever possible, the words of each folksong have been included with corresponding paraphrases or translations. The atmosphere, and often the significance of each song, is indicated by the setting in which it is performed.

Part One of the book deals with the principles of Indian folk music, covering the various components in turn. To be performed effectively, the songs should always be accompanied by an instrumental combination of some form or other, including some percussion. Unless otherwise stated, the songs should also be accompanied by dance, to be performed by those not involved in the music-making. Truly authentic Indian dance can only be mastered with in-depth study of the genre; improvisation, however, is common and dance movements and styles diverse. The guidance offered is designed to enable you to achieve a suitably effective result, and you should feel free to improvise further.

The folksongs themselves, forming Part Two, come from the north (Uttar Pradesh), the east (Bengal), the south (Mysore) and the west (Gujarat), each area having its own distinctive set of cultural traditions. The chord symbols are designed to assist in the learning of the melody, and to aid performance when sufficient percussion/melody instruments are unavailable.

As with folksongs the world over, there exist many different versions of each song. For this collection I have tried to find the most well-known.

Acknowledgements

I am indebted to the following people, all of whom gave me invaluable help with the selection and preparation of the folksongs, in particular with the text: Dharmendra Bhatt, Muhammad Ajmal Ali, Perwin Rahman and her daughters Sumona and Romana. Also to the eminent violinist and composer Chandra Sekhara, who gave me a new perspective on Indian music.

Peter Gritton

Contents

Part One: The Principles of Indian Music

The Drone	1
The Tala	2
Percussion	3
Melody	5
Melodic instruments	6
Improvisation	6
Pronunciation	6

Part Two: Twenty Indian Folksongs

Morning dance	8
Drum song	9
Dance with sticks	10
Dancing with gourds	11
The flute	12
Wedding song	13
Gananayaka	14
Allah	15
Dance of the mother goddess	16
Krishna	17
Krishna's prank	18
Festive song	19
The parrot man	20
Come on, man!	21
The palki	22
Chandamama!	23
Evening song	24
Moon dance	25
The way of life	26
Shiva's dance	28

Part One: The Principles of Indian Music

There are several ingredients which, when put together, provide the basic sounds of Indian 'classical' music, which in turn forms the basis for Indian 'folk' music.

The Drone

The drone is a sustained note or collection of notes providing a foundation on which the songs are then performed. Along with drum accompaniment and the 'tala' (see below), it is generally a constant feature of all Indian folksongs and should be played continuously unless indicated otherwise. In 'classical' music the drone's purpose is largely atmospheric, but in folksong its continuous nature helps singers stay in tune and in time. The most commonly-used drone instrument is the large, lute-like 'tambura', which you can simulate using a guitar. For a more continuous sound, Indians use the harmonium or the hand-organ, swelling from soft to loud with the mood of the music. Using the 'circular breathing' technique, Indian musicians also play an instrument called the 'shehnai' to produce a continuous note. You can simulate this with, for example, two bassoonists breathing alternately. A bowed cello note is also effective. Try any combination of instruments available, using a keyboard only if you have to.

Exercises for plucked instruments (or keyboard):

1.

2.

3.

4.

5.

6.

Exercises for sustaining instruments:

Harmonium/organ, or similar

1.
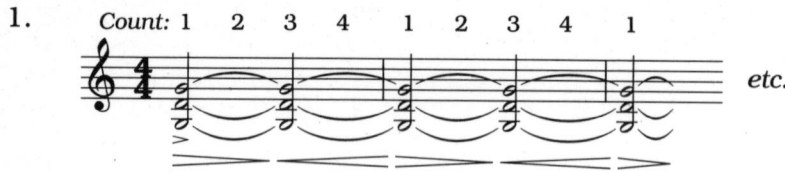

2.
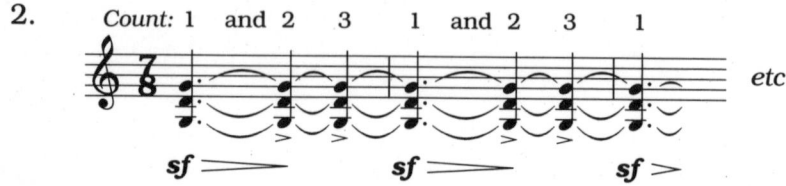

Bassoon/cello, or similar

3.

Lower notes optional – div. or 'double stop' (cello)

Throughout the volume the plucked drone style is given, though you should feel free to support a plucked drone with a sustained one at will. If a plucked instrument is not available, take the main note or notes of the plucked drone and sustain them.

The Tala

The 'Tala' (or 'taal') is the rhythmic movement and gesture used by dancers to reinforce the underlying rhythm of a folksong. The word itself has become synonymous with clapping and comes from 'ta', the dance of the god Shiva, and 'la', the dance of his lady companion. Clapping and dancing are an integral part of Indian folk music.

Some talas are easier to learn than others; a few are given below, starting with the simpler ones. The cross (×) indicates a clap, a click of the fingers or the tapping together of two sticks. The circle (o) indicates a wave or silent gesture, such as putting your hands out in front of you or to the side (a symbol of sharing with others). You should note that it is more authentic not to clap or tap too loudly, unless the mood is excited. In some cases, Indian folk musicians simply put their hands together silently. Except in quicker tempo songs, all movements should be flowing and graceful. Practise the following 'talas' at a variety of speeds, repeating each many times. In order to maintain a steady rhythm, count the pulse as you practise each tala. Alternatively, you could use a soft drum, or tap the pulse on some other percussion instrument.

1. Tintaal (16 beats)

```
Count:  1   2   3   4  | 5   6   7   8  |
        ×                ×
       (clap)           (clap)


        9  10  11  12  | 13  14  15  16 | etc.
        o                ×
       (wave)           (clap)
```

2. Kherwa tala (4 beats)

Count: 1 2 3 4 | 1 2 3 4 | etc.
        x   o   x   o

3. Adi tala (8 beats)

Count: 1 2 3 4 | 5 6 7 8 | etc.
        x   x o x o

4. Dadra tal (6 beats)

Count: 1 2 3 | 4 5 6 | etc.
        x   o

5. Rupak tal (7 beats)

Count: 1 2 3 4 5 6 7 | etc.
        o   x   x

Once you have mastered these at slow, medium and fast speeds, *and* in a sequence which gradually gets faster, add the talas to the drones: drones 1 and 2 combine with talas 1, 2 and 3, so try each of these rhythms with either one of the drones. Do not go any further until you can comfortably combine these drones and talas.

NB. Maintain relaxed wrists at all times: keep the face relaxed and smile!

Now try drones 3 and 4 with tala 4. When you feel really at ease with this, try drones 5 and 6 with tala 5. Talas are fundamental to Indian folk music, so it is well worth the challenge of learning them and then adding them to the music while you sing and dance. The aim is to be relaxed but rhythmic. Throughout the book there are performance suggestions showing you how to use talas and drones which, when combined with percussion and melody, create the magical Indian sound.

Percussion

Indian percussion instruments are numerous and varied. The most common are the 'tabla' – two drums of different sizes tied together with gut or string and used principally in 'classical' Indian music. The folk equivalent is the double-headed 'dholak', which may either be a single drum with skin across both ends, or look like a tabla. Indian drummers improvise around the underlying rhythm of the song, while the drone and tala continue throughout without alteration. Below are some written out 'improvisations' which should be performed along with the tala rhythms. These 'dholak' improvisations, usually performed by one or two skilled players, have been divided here between a group of drummers.

1.

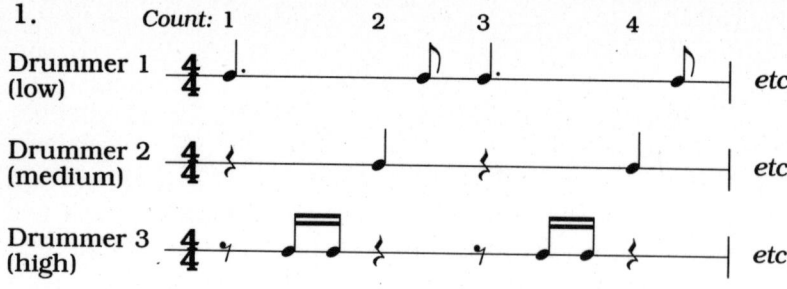

2.

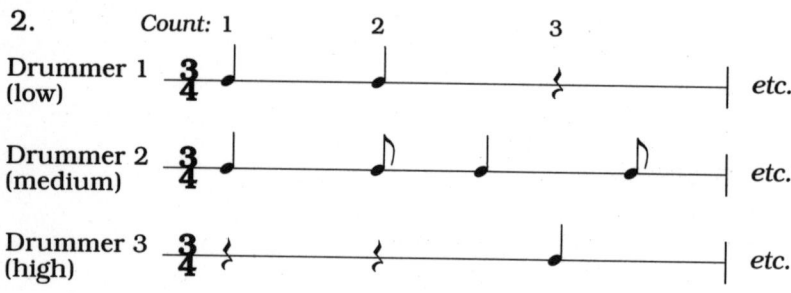

Additional part for improvisatory effect when singers stop:

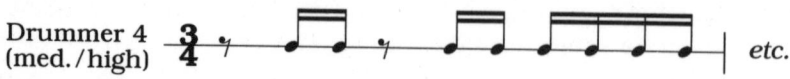

In 1 and 2 count a whole bar ('cycle') before the entry of drummer 1. This rhythm should be repeated until the drummer's playing is steady and rhythmic. Then add drummer 2, thus starting a building process. When both drummers together achieve rhythmic stability add drummer 3, and in turn drummer 4. Continue this rhythmic soundpiece for several minutes until the atmosphere is relaxed. Drones and talas may then be added: you will see that drones 1 and 2, and therefore talas 1, 2 and 3, can be added to the first drum pattern, and that tala 4 and drones 3 and 4 can be added to the second. It could be helpful to write out the drone/tala/drum patterns together so that the performers can see the way they combine.

The following improvisation uses the 7-beat cycle. Once you have set up the patterns of each drummer and achieved the characteristic Indian feel, it may be an idea to play the tala on a triangle, thus imitating the 'manjira' (hand cymbals) sometimes used by dancers. This will help stabilise the uneven pulse. Tala 5 and drones 5 and 6 fit with this third drum pattern.

3.

These rhythmic ideas should prove invaluable as you work on the songs in this book, and you should also freely vary the rhythms suggested with each song. For example, in the third pattern, instead of playing:

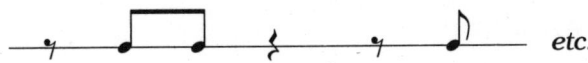 etc.

drummer 3 can play:

 etc.

Along with the drone and tala, drumming should generally be constant throughout every song, i.e. during choruses, dances and instrumental-only sections. Drummers tend to improvise more freely when the singers are silent. The intensity of a song can be heightened during these instrumental interludes, the dancers also improvising in response to the more excited mood. A song usually ends with a strike from the drummers on the first beat of the bar following the final note of the melody.

As well as the 'tabla' or 'dholak', many other instruments are used for rhythm: 'keratala' – a large bell-like instrument played with sticks; 'lejama' – bamboo poles with iron rings on the end, played by shaking; and 'supa' – upturned woven baskets strummed with the fingers. It is up to you what you use; as well as more conventional percussion instruments, you might also freely adapt everyday equipment around you to produce sounds appropriate to Indian village street music!

Melody

Whereas 'classical' Indian melodies are based on systems known as 'ragas', and are often angular and awkward to sing, folksongs are generally more straightforward, and thus simpler for non-Indians to imitate. It is not easy, however, to recreate the unmistakable Indian vocal timbre – achieved by the use of vibrato, melisma, and ornamentation. For the purposes of this collection it is perfectly acceptable to sing the songs 'straight', though the following is an example of the way in which an Indian singer might actually sing a melody:

Many notes are preceded by an anticipatory 'grace' note (**A**); slow vibrato is often used to decorate longer notes (**B**); and melismas are usually performed smoothly to create a flowing, snake-like sound (**C**).

Melodic instruments

Melodic instruments are used to double the singers and to play instrumental interludes. Use a guitar to imitate the traditional 'sitar' and a violin for the 'sarangi'. (The violin itself was imported from the west centuries ago, and is regarded as traditional in Indian music.) The most common instrument for solos is the flute – use either a flute or recorder. Beyond this you should freely experiment with sounds of other Western instruments for melody. Some combinations can produce startlingly 'ethnic' results.

Improvisation

It is possible to take your performance of the songs a stage further through improvisation, so that a short song becomes a dramatic structure lasting anywhere from 5 minutes to 20! Experiment with your own performance ideas using the suggestions provided as a basis. Indian musicians will often continue a folksong after a climax is reached, so that it builds up again from a soft beginning:

slow → accel → fast ‖ slow → accel → fast *etc.*

Pronunciation

Although truly authentic Indian pronunciation requires many detailed subtleties, there are only a few points to be made for the purposes of the songs in this collection. As a general rule the pronunciation is phonetic except for *v*, pronounced *w*: 'bhavani' = ba-wa-nee. *Bh*, *dh*, *kh*, *jh*, *th*, etc. are best pronounced *b*, *d*, *k*, *j* and *t* respectively. *Ch* is an exception and is pronounced as in cheese. The combination of vowels *ai* or *ay* sound like the English word 'eye'; *ei* sounds as in the English word 'day'. *Aa* and *a* can be treated as the same.

Part Two: Twenty Indian Folksongs

Morning dance

Gujarat

This song is traditionally performed in the early morning to the god 'Saraswati'. The bouncing rhythms in the first line are designed to wake up everybody – including Saraswati!

Performance:
Introduction (2 bars), Instrumental (8),
Drum/dance interlude (16), Instrumental (8), Chorus (4),
Instrumental (4), Chorus (4), Drums (4).

The song should begin slowly and quietly, using drums and drone for the introduction. On each repeat of the instrumental section, instruments may be added: for example, use a solo flute accompanied by soft drums and drone for the first, then add a violin or guitar for the next repeat; include all available instruments for the final four-bar interlude. In the drum/dance interlude, begin to get faster and louder. The dancing may continue to the end of the song. By the time you reach the first chorus the song should be quite loud. The second chorus is stronger still, and is followed by a final four-bar drum passage, finishing as emphatically as possible.

Drone

Drums

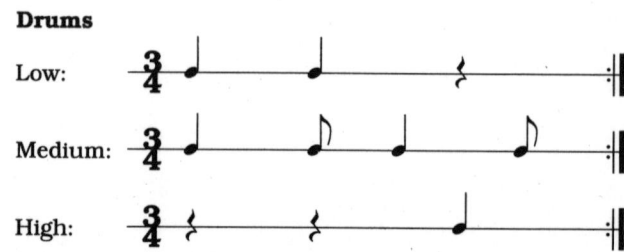

© 1993 by Faber Music Ltd. This music is copyright. Photocopying is illegal.

Drum song

Mysore

Tay-a tay-a-ta, tay-a tay-a-ta, da da da da da da din din da. Ho—

tay-a tay-a-ta, tay-a tay-a-ta, da da da da da da din din da, din da da din da da da da da da,

din din day-a day-a da da da. Ho— tay-a tay-a-ta, Ho— tay-a tay-a-ta.

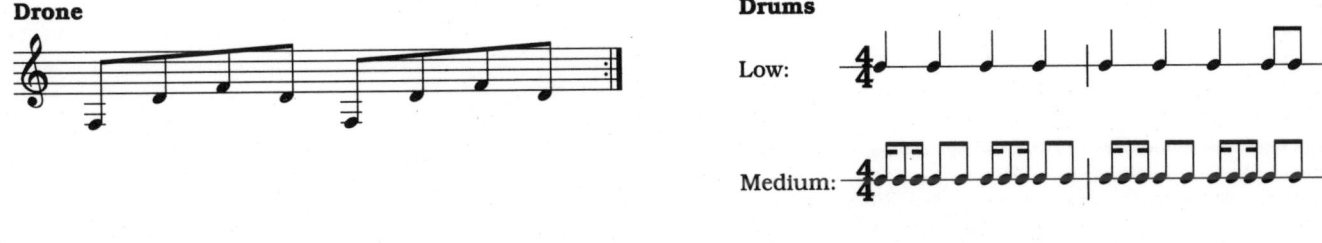

The words of this amusing song are based on drum sounds! Indians use all kinds of syllables to describe various ways of hitting a drum – generally known as 'bol' sounds. Aim for a really happy, lively sound!

Performance:
Introduction (6 bars), Melody (8), 'Drum dance' (8), Melody (16).

Begin the introduction with low drum and drone; add medium drum after 2 bars, and high after 4. Work out a dance pattern incorporating movements made when hitting drums. A fourth drum can be added for the dance, using a rhythm such as:

When the melody is repeated towards the end this rhythm may return for extra excitement. Accompany the voices with melody instruments only if you need to.

Dance with sticks

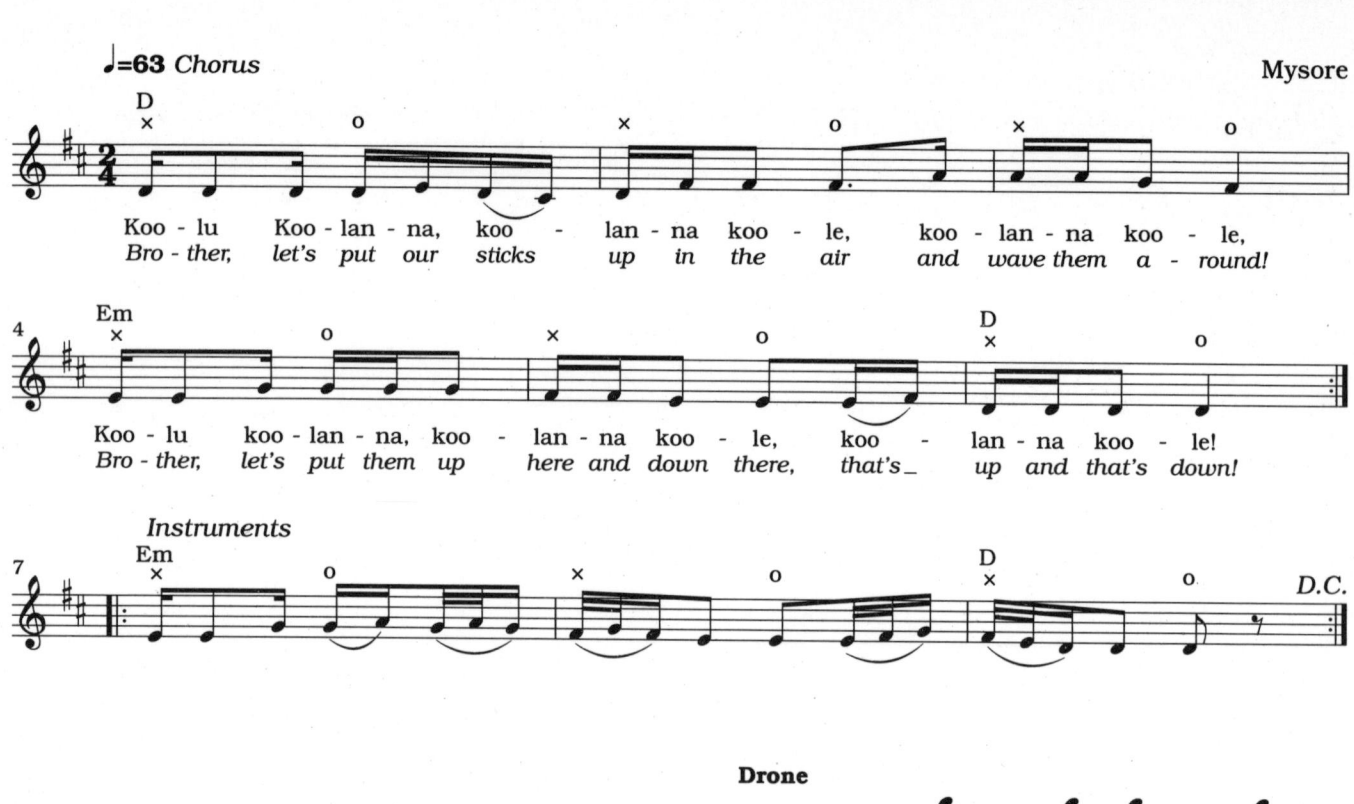

Mysore

♩=63 *Chorus*

Koo - lu Koo - lan - na, koo - lan - na koo - le, koo - lan - na koo - le,
Bro - ther, let's put our sticks up in the air and wave them a - round!

Koo - lu koo - lan - na, koo - lan - na koo - le, koo - lan - na koo - le!
Bro - ther, let's put them up here and down there, that's__ up and that's down!

Instruments

Drone

Drums

Low:
Medium:
High:

Dancers are commonly seen with sticks in their hands. They tap them above their heads and draw beautiful shapes in the air with them.

Performance:
Introduction (6 bars), Chorus (12), Instrumental (6), Chorus (12), 'Stick dance' (as long as you wish), Instrumental (6), Chorus (repeat ad lib).

For the introduction, begin with the low drum, adding the other drums and drone after 3 bars. Double the chorus with instruments if necessary. Use several instruments or just a solo oboe or flute/recorder (up an octave) for the instrumental sections. Work out a 'stick dance', each dancer holding two short sticks which he or she taps and waves as the dance progresses. The dance may continue to the end of the song. The final 'chorus' should get faster and faster, creating a frenzied finish!

Dancing with gourds

Gujarat

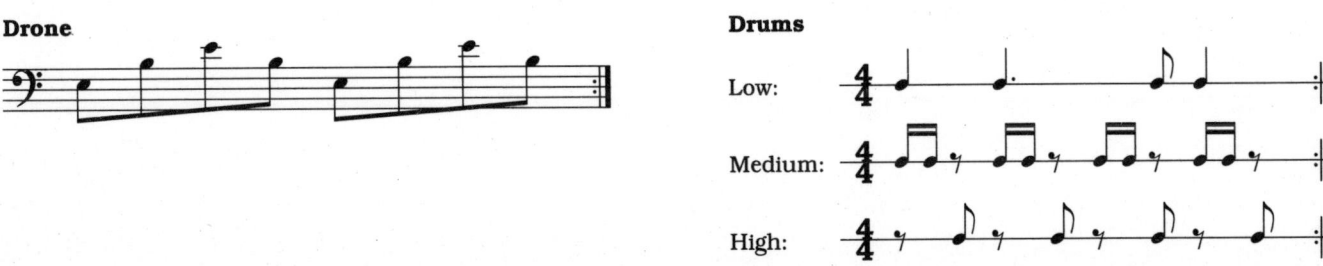

This is an enchanting folksong depicting the gathering of young gods playing amongst themselves. As in so many Indian folksongs, the gods virtually walk among the people, here in the form of children. In this song, the gods are playing with hollow gourds, perhaps placing them on their heads and dancing around Chacharna (the name of the place).

Performance:
*Introduction (4 bars), Chorus (8),
Instrumental interlude (8), Chorus (8),
Drums/drone 'link' (2),
Dance interlude (16), Chorus (8).*

Try an introduction made up of 2 bars of low drum solo, joined by medium and high drums, and drone for the next 2 bars. Double the voices with soft-sounding instruments, but for the instrumental interlude use perhaps an oboe or saxophone. The dance interlude should be accompanied by 8 bars 'chorus' followed by 8 bars 'instrumental interlude', played on flutes and recorders. The final chorus would be effective sung strongly with the addition of the oboe to the instrumental ensemble.

The flute

The sound of an Indian snake-charmer – as often seen in Indian films – is always magical and haunting. This melody is based on a South Indian folk tune, and is best performed without a drone.

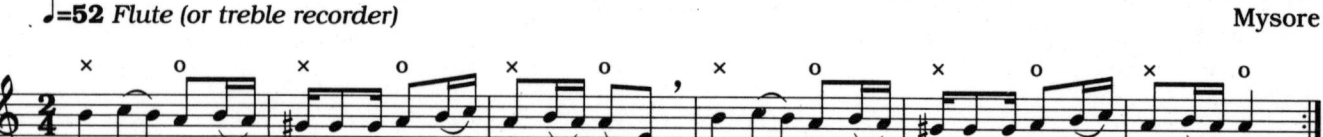

Mysore

Performance:
Introduction (6 bars), Flute (as many repeats as you wish), Drum interlude (6), Flute (12).

Begin the introduction with low drum only, adding medium and high after 3 bars. The drums continue to the end of the piece. Use the winding, repetitive flute melody as the inspiration for a 'snake dance' – either with a dancer, or group of dancers imitating a snake being coaxed out of a basket, or by pulling a 'snake' out of a basket on a piece of cotton so that it looks alive!

Drums

Low:

Medium:

High:

Wedding song

Uttar Pradesh

Performance:
Melody as introduction (4 bars), Drums (4), Poem with drum accompaniment (as many bars as necessary), Add drone (2), Add melody (16 bars).

Sing the melody once, slowly and unaccompanied, as an introduction, pausing on the last note. Then begin the drum accompaniment with 4 bars of medium drum joined by low and high drum after 2 bars. The poem can be read (and acted) by a collection of readers. When the poem has been completed, add the drone to the drums and finish the song with the melody sung four times, getting faster each time.

This traditional wedding song is based on the following poem:

> The queen's palace has been
>   painted green and yellow
> With cowdung and mud.
> On top of the palace
>   sits a crow on a pole.
> "Oh crow, I'll give you a present
> if you fetch my brother", the bride said.
> Before the crow could answer,
>   along came her brother.
> Her brother brought gifts,
>   but even then he was rejected
> By her husband's family.
> Someone was rude to him,
>   so he turned and left.
> 'How could I stop my brother leaving
> When my hands and
>   feet were *painted?
> Oh paint, go away, so I can tell him to
> Ask my husband:
> "Please, please let
>   my sister come home".'
>
>   (paraphrased)

*The body is painted for marriage ceremonies.

The poem goes on to list the things a bride is instructed to do by the groom's family: in the month of Savana, she should play with dolls! In the month of Bhadau they complete worship. In the following month, they should fast for nine days and nights (the festival 'Navatri'), then bathe in the Ganges.

Gananayaka

Mysore

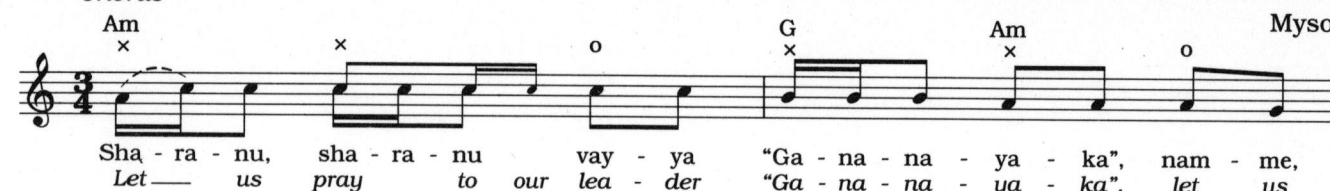

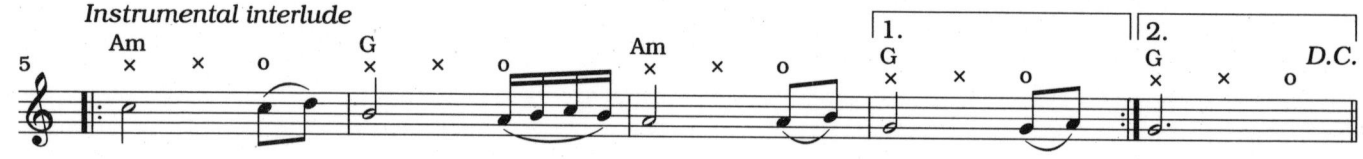

'Gananayaka' is the name of the all-powerful Hindu god, and in this song he is worshipped by the people through 'Shambu' – similar to Christian worship of God through Jesus Christ.

Performance:
Introduction (8 bars), Sung melody (8), Interlude (8), Sung melody (8), Drums/drone 'link' (4), Dance interlude with solo flute/recorder (as long as you wish), Sung melody (8), Interlude (8), Sung melody (8).

Try introducing the song using a solo flute or recorder playing the interlude material. The drums, drone and any doubling instruments can begin together at the same time as the first sung melody. The drums/drone 'link' is to allow you time to get into position for dancing, and for focussing on the solo flute/recorder. After the dance interlude, the drums/drone can enter quietly with the voices, gradually getting louder, while the dancing continues to the end. The song can get faster during the last 24 bars.

Drone

Drums

Allah

Bengal

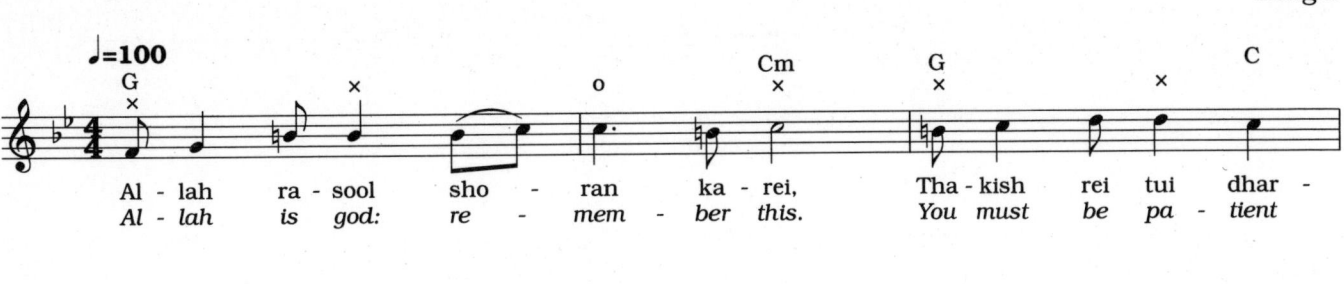

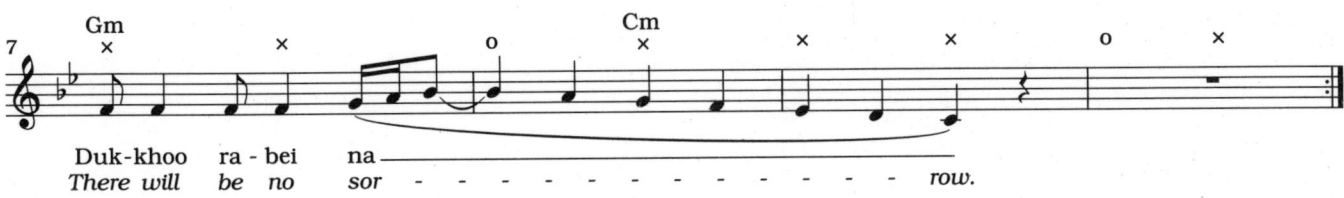
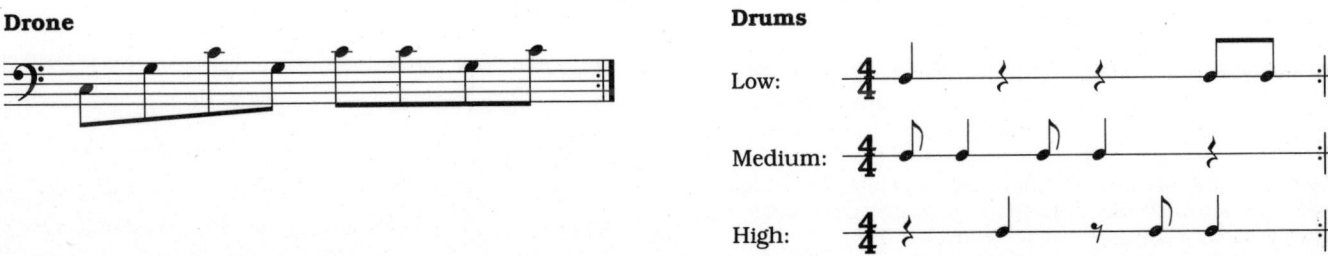

Allah is the god worshipped by Muslims in their religion, Islam. This religious song celebrates the rewards of praying to Allah.

Performance:
Introduction (2 bars), Instrumental melody (10), Sung melody (10), Dance Interlude (as long as you wish), Instrumental melody (10), Sung melody (10).

Try a short introduction with all three drummers and the drone starting together. Use any available instruments – recorders, flutes, violins etc. for the melody, doubling an octave higher if you wish. You could try a dance interlude, accompanied by drumming, allowing you to try out some simple dance routines – for example, walking slowly in a circle, while performing a 'tala' with sticks (see Part One). This interlude also offers an opportunity for some drum improvisation, for example:

Keep the low drum the same, and don't forget that you can add a fourth drummer if you wish.

— 15 —

Dance of the mother goddess

Gujarat

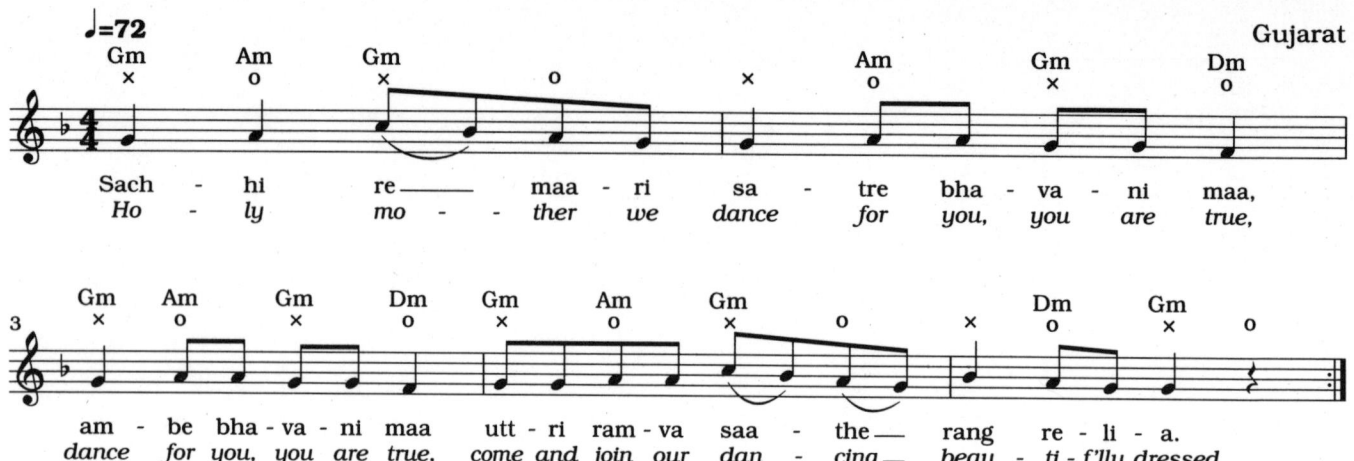

Sach - hi re — maa - ri sa - tre bha - va - ni maa,
Ho - ly mo - - ther we dance for you, you are true,

am - be bha - va - ni maa utt - ri ram - va saa - the — rang re - li - a.
dance for you, you are true, come and join our dan - cing — beau - ti - f'lly dressed.

This song celebrates the virtues of the 'Mother Goddess'. It is usually performed with vocal ornaments and melismas – not easily imitated by Westerners. If sung simply – but with passion – you will create a similar mood. In India, imaginative dances are performed to tunes such as this; the words suggest a large circle of girls (satre=seventeen) symbolising mother goddesses coming down to earth in colourful dresses and joining the people in song and dance.

Performance:
Introduction (2 bars), Melody with voices (5), Melody on instruments (5), Dance of the Mother Goddess (as long as you wish), Melody on instruments (5), Melody with voices and instruments (5).

Introduce the melody with the drone and all drums. Only add instruments to the melody line if the singers need support. The instruments may then answer the voices by repeating the melody alone. The words can be used to inspire some imaginative, colourful dancing, which should be accompanied by drums and drone. The dancing may continue to the end.

Drone

Drums

Low:

Medium:

High:

— 16 —

Krishna

♩=108　　　　　　　　　　　　　　　　　　　　　　　　　　　　　　　　　Mysore

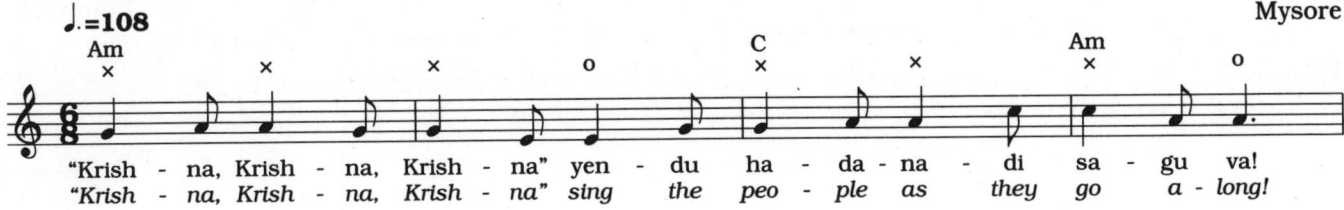

"Krish - na, Krish - na, Krish - na" yen - du ha - da - na - di sa - gu va!
"Krish - na, Krish - na, Krish - na" sing the peo - ple as they go a - long!

"Krish - na, Krish - na, Krish - na" yen - du ha - da - na - di ba - lu va!
"Krish - na, Krish - na, Krish - na" let this chant for ev - er be our song!

Performance:
Introduction (4 bars), Chorus (16), Drum improvisation with dance (32), Chorus (repeat ad lib).

Begin the introduction with drums and drone together, setting up the rhythm and pitch for the chorus. For the drum improvisation use rhythms such as:

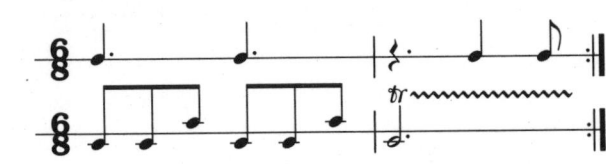

and

When the chorus returns, continue with the dancing and these improvised rhythms to maintain the excited mood. Get faster with each repeat, and finish very strongly (not forgetting that the final strike of the drums is on the first beat of a bar!)

Drone

Drums

Low:

Medium/high
(*one player*):

Krishna is one of the most popular Hindu gods and is often portrayed as a child who performs mischievous deeds (see *Krishna's Prank* and *Festive Song*). He also works miracles and appears as a romantic lover.

— 17 —

Krishna's prank

Uttar Pradesh

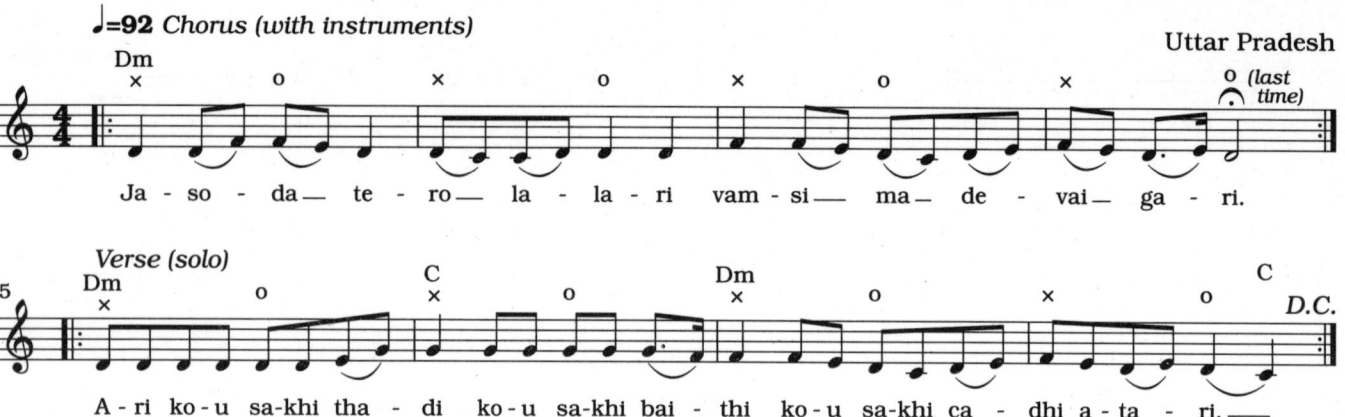

Ja - so - da - te - ro - la - la - ri vam - si - ma - de - vai - ga - ri.

A - ri ko - u sa - khi tha - di ko - u sa - khi bai - thi ko - u sa - khi ca - dhi a - ta - ri,

Both *Krishna's Prank* and *Festive Song* (page 19) are based on a well-known traditional Indian story, paraphrased below. The complete texts of both songs are long and complicated, so just the first few lines are given here. Indian religious figures are often connected with every-day life – here in the form of Krishna, who plays pranks with the village folk! At the end of the poem there is a typical Aesop-like moral – make of it what you will!

"Krishna, give back our clothes!
There you are, Krishna, sitting in a tree, and
Here we are naked in the water.
I can't go back to my husband's family
Because they will be really angry.
The milkmaid is calling me from the other side
And I am on this side of the river still.
Look, Krishna, I have even got a heavy waterpot
On my head.
Everybody's going to laugh at me and clap their hands."
Krishna says, "I will give you your clothes, oh milkmaid,
Come out of the river."
Surdas says, "I came to meet you; You won and I lost."

Performance:
Introduction (8 bars), *Chorus* (8), *Verse* (8), *Chorus* (8), *Poem* (as many bars as necessary), *Chorus* (8), *Verse* (8), *Chorus* (8). (As for Festive Song.)

Drone

Drums

Low:

Medium:

High:

Festive song

Uttar Pradesh

♩=108 *Chorus (with instruments)*

Ka - hi ka - ra pri - ta - ma pi - a - re ka-

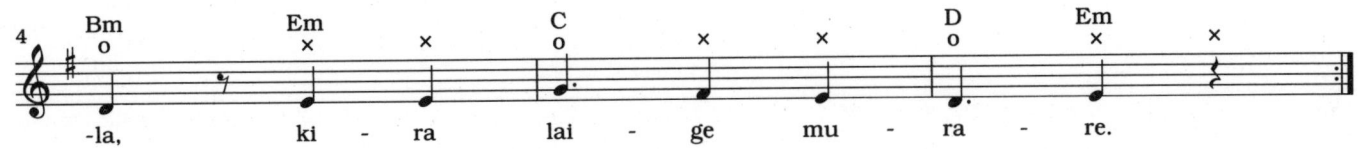

-la, ki - ra lai - ge mu - ra - re.

Verse (solo)

Lai - ke ki - ra Ka - da - ma ca - dhi bai - the.

Performance:
Introduction (8 bars), Chorus (12), Verse (8), Chorus (12), Poem (as many bars as necessary), Chorus (12), Verse (8), Chorus (12).

Introducing the drums one by one, at two bar intervals (low, medium, then high), followed by the drone makes an effective 8-bar introduction. The poem may be read in the middle of the performance, accompanied by quiet, repetitive drumming with or without the drone.

Drone

Drums

The parrot man

Mysore

Gee - ju - ga gi - ni Ra - ma nee — Ra - ma nee Ra - ghu Ra - ma nee. —
There is a par - rot - man and he — tells his par - rot "You Ra - ma be." —

This song is of the amusing situation of a man telling his parrot, which sits on his shoulder, that it is the mouthpiece of Rama, a Hindu god. The fact that a parrot can imitate human speech has perhaps influenced this song – its voice is supposed to have been founded among the gods.

Performance:
Introduction (2 bars), Chorus (8), Interlude (6), Chorus (8), Dance (as long as you wish), Interlude (6), Chorus (8).

The introduction can be made up of drums and drone together. Use a mixture of instruments to double the voices and for the instrumental interlude (e.g. flute, recorder, violin, guitar and/or oboe). For the dance simply use drone and drums. The parrot could influence the dance – one person, or a group of people imitating another like a parrot. The dance may continue into the interlude, finishing in time for the final chorus.

Drone

Drums

Come on, man!

Mysore

Come on, Man! is sung by a group of people affectionately encouraging someone else to join them. It should be sung in a friendly way, even when the man is called a 'silly parrot' – think of this as a term of endearment!

Performance:
Introduction (16 bars), Chorus (16), Instrumental interlude (8), Chorus (16), Drums and drone (4), Chorus (16).

This song could be sung to a scene in which a group of people doing some activity gradually persuade someone else to come and join them. The 16-bar introduction may be used to set the scene, then one of the crowd steps forward and sings the melody to the loner. During the instrumental interlude, the loner moves closer, more singers from the crowd encouraging him/her in the ensuing chorus. In the drums/drone interlude, the individual joins the crowd in time to sing the final chorus with everyone.

Drone

Drums

Low:

Medium/high
(*one player*):

The palki

Bengal

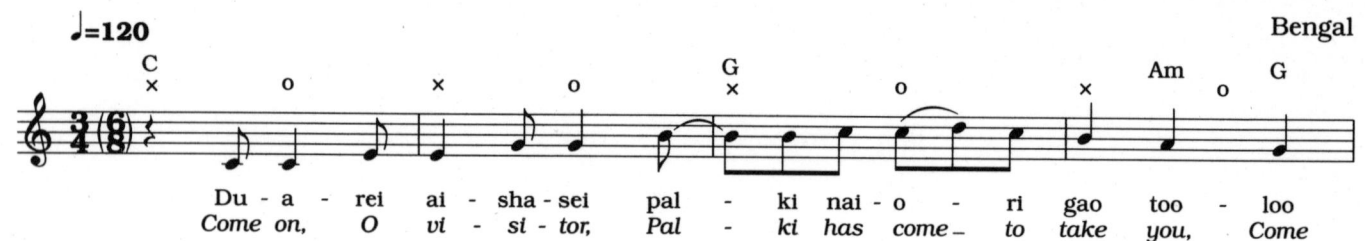

The 'palki' is a type of carriage used to carry away the dead. It is also used for weddings, and in this case it is used to carry a visitor. There could be some significance, however, in the use of the palki for a visitor in this instance – a possible subject for discussion.

Performance:
*Introduction (3 bars), Chorus (18 bars),
Instrumental interlude (18),
Drum 'link' (3), Chorus (18).*

The introduction should be made up of drums and drone in a steady rhythm. The voices may be doubled with a guitar and/or violin. For the instrumental interlude, simply play the melody on a solo flute or recorder first time (up an octave), adding guitar and/or violin on the repeat. The 3-bar drum 'link' can get faster, with the final chorus performed 'tutti' at the faster speed.

Chandamama!

♩=116 Chorus (with instruments)

Mysore

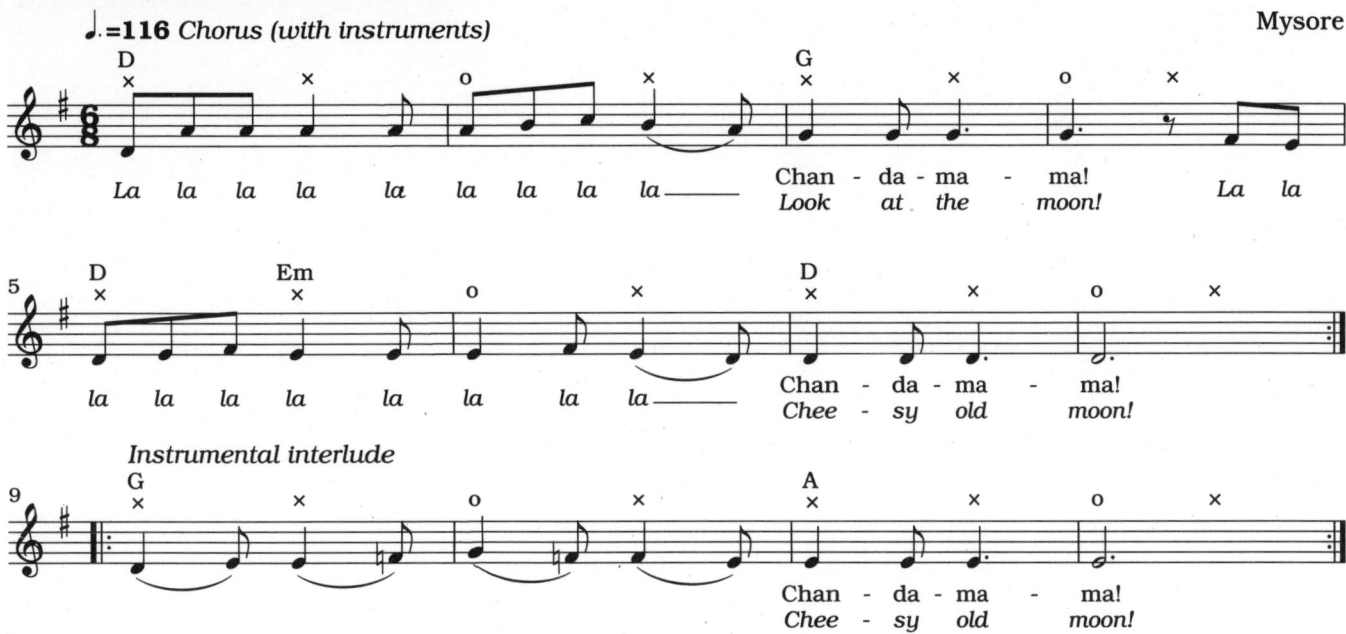

Children in Mysore refer to the moon as 'Chandamama'.

Performance:
Chorus (8 bars), Drums and drone (4), Chorus (16),
Instrumental interlude (8), Chorus (8), 'Dance to the
moon' (as long as you wish), Chorus (16),
Instrumental interlude (8), Chorus (8).

Drone

Drums

Begin with the chorus played by melody instruments (without drums and drone), the voices just singing the word 'Chandamama'. In all subsequent choruses the voices sing the notes set to 'la' as well as 'Chandamama'. From their entry in bar 9, the drums and drone should play emphatically to the end of the piece. The voices should sing the words 'Chandamama' within the instrumental interludes. The 'Dance to the moon' should be accompanied by drums and drone only.

— 23 —

Evening song
Gujarat

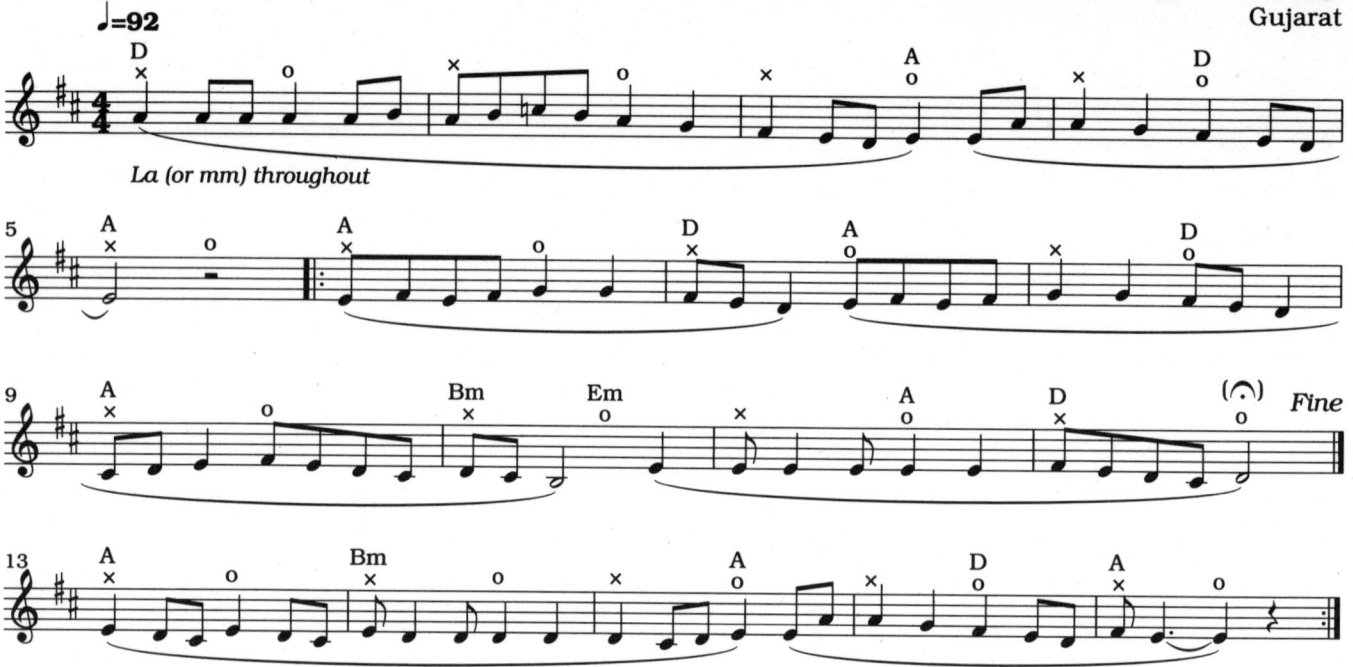

La (or mm) throughout

This song is sung at evening prayer, particularly during the nine-day ceremony 'Navatri'. There is also a reference to this with *Wedding Song* (page 13).

Performance:
Introduction (2 bars),
Melody with repeat, to 'Fine' (24 bars).

The drums and drone should begin together, joined by the sung melody as written, with soft instrumental accompaniment (eg. violin and/or guitar). You can create a peaceful mood if the performers all sit in a circle, for example. They could also join hands.

Drone

Drums

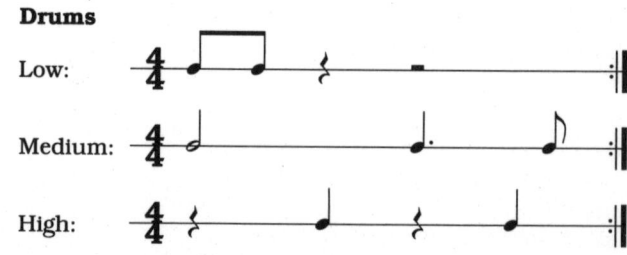

Moon dance

Gujarat

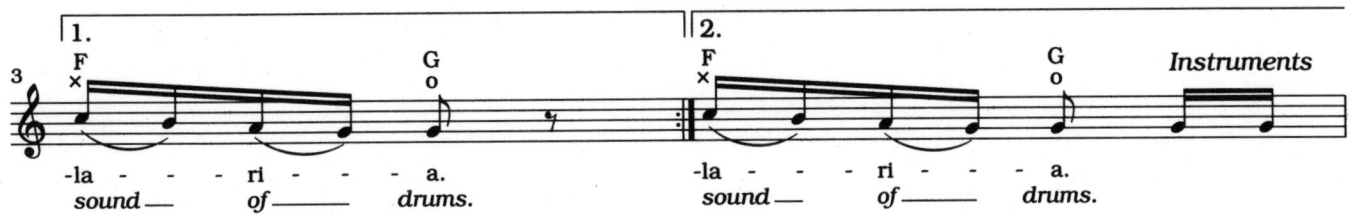

Last time

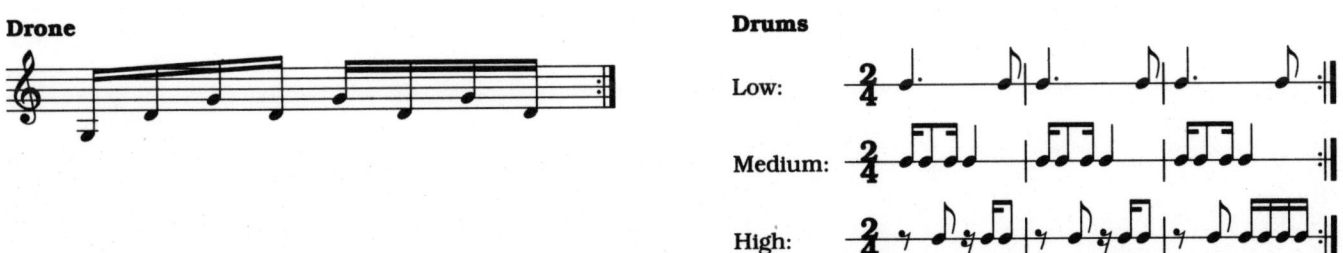

This is an atmospheric song and should be performed with much expression. There are folksongs for all times of the day – this one is for night-time.

Performance:
Introduction (6 bars), Chorus (6), Instrumental interlude (6), Chorus (6), Drum dance (as long as you wish), Chorus (6), Instrumental interlude (6), Chorus (6), Instrumental interlude (repeat ad lib).

Use the instrumental interlude, played by solo flute or recorder (6 bars) as an introduction, adding low drum and drone after the first 3 bars. The first chorus can be accompanied by low drum and drone, in order to save the exciting sound of all the drums playing together for the drum dance. From the drum dance to the end, use all the drums together; the dancing may continue to the end of the song. Use any combination of instruments for the instrumental interlude. For the final section, add an instrument on each repeat, getting faster each time, so that the song ends *presto* and **ff**.

The way of life

Bengal

Most of the songs in this collection are short and are commonly repeated many times in performance. The Way of Life, however, is like an endless yarn, weaving in unexpected directions. It must be sung with much feeling, especially in the higher passages.

Performance:
Introduction (4 bars),
Sung melody (complete),
Instrumental melody (complete),
Melody sung and played (complete).

The sung melody should contrast strongly with the final rendition with instruments, though it may none-the-less be accompanied quietly the first time through. For the instrumental version try any combination available – it is effective either played unison on several instruments or as a solo for flute or recorder.

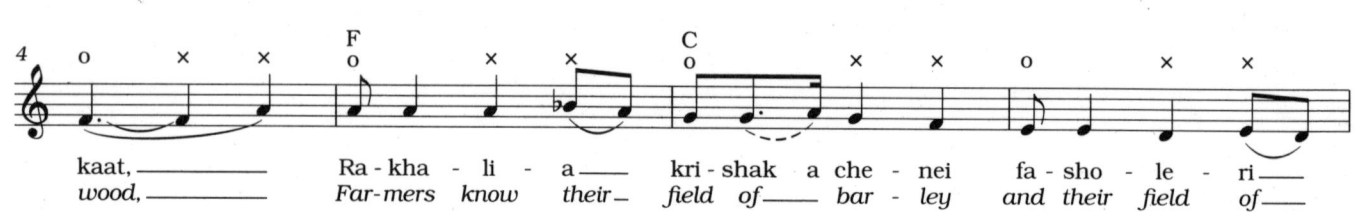

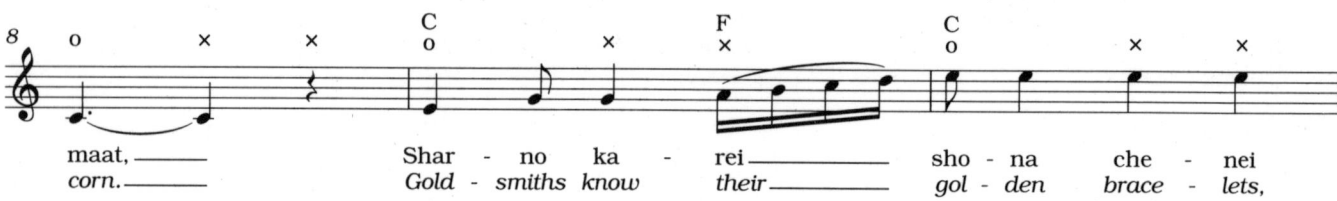

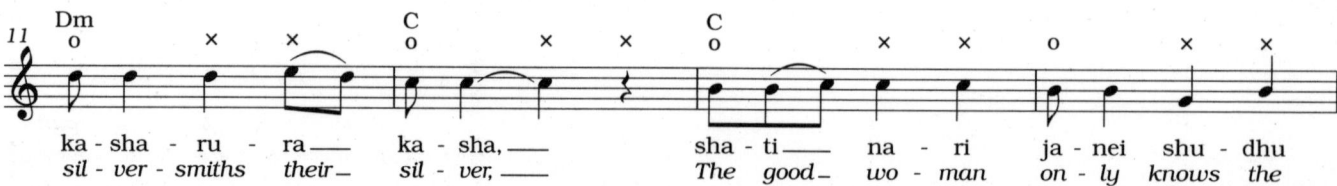

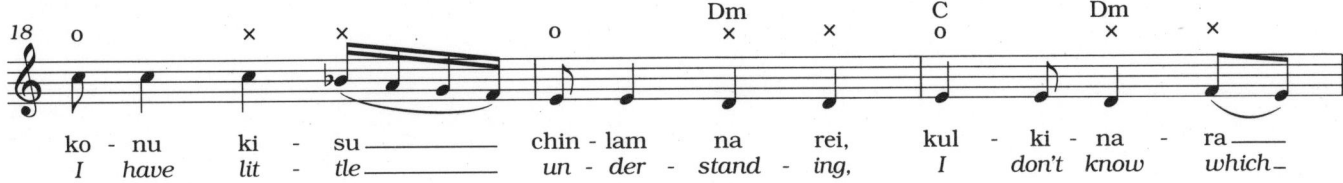
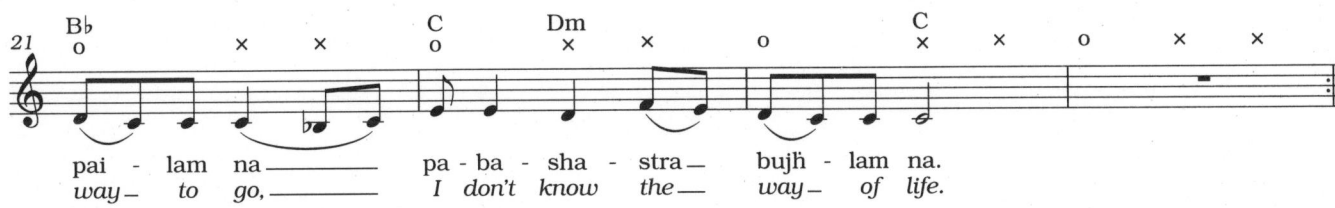

Drone

Drums

Low:

Medium:

High:

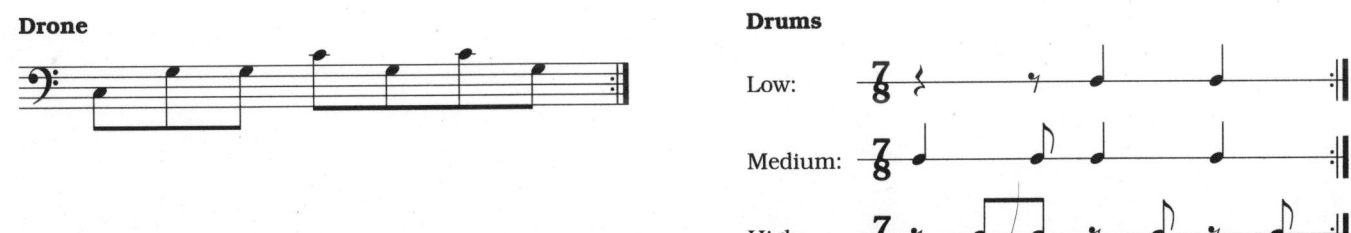

—27—

Shiva's dance

Nothing moves till Shiva moves. When Shiva dances everything dances. When Shiva dances, you dance ... and dance ... and dance ... until you drop.

Ancient Indian texts speak of Shiva, the god of all, and his dancing companion, Parvati. *Shiva's dance* is a 'chain' of dances, in 6/8 and 2/4 respectively, each of which starts softly and slowly building up to a loud, fast climax. This type of 'progressive' dance is a tradition stretching back thousands of years, and is commonly seen in India today. As the dance becomes more and more ecstatic, the performers are liberated from their minds' control. To the ear it is as if each new dance begins before the old one has completely died away.

Performance:
Begin Dance 1 at ♩.=c.60, with the medium drum playing:

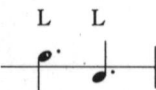

before breaking into the suggested rhythm. Then add the low drum, followed by the high drum. After four repeats, gradually begin to get faster. After a further four repeats (you should have reached ♩.=c.100) add the melody on flute and/or recorders. Continue to repeat the melody, increasing the tempo, and when the speed is approximately ♩.=144, the dancers (who have been dancing throughout) shout "Shiva", "Parvati" several times, as given. At the point of climax, everything stops except the medium drum, which continues with Dance 2, and the whole process is repeated.

Dance 1

Melody instruments

Dance 2

Melody instruments

Drums

Low:

Medium: (2 drums)
High: (2 drums)

Drums

Low:

Medium: (2 drums)
High: (2 drums)

Voices (for 'climax' of dances only)

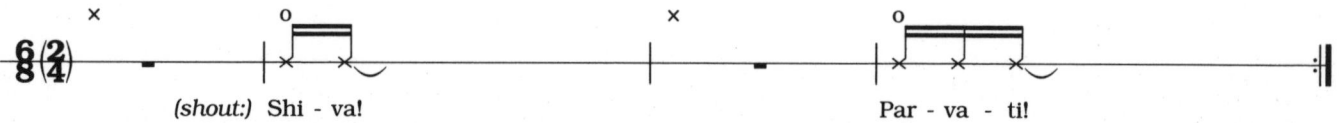

Printed by
Halstan & Co. Ltd., Amersham, Bucks., England